Did I Write a Poem Once?

A Collection of Poems

Sue Bates

First printed edition 2017

The Bothy Publishing
Terreran Bothy
Main Street
Gartmore
Scotland
FK8 3RN

www.bothy-publishing.com
enquiries@bothy-publishing

cover design by Sue Bates
ISBN 978-0-9929124-6-8

CONTENTS

THE POEMS
In chronological order (mostly)

INTRODUCTION

When a friend of mine died recently I knew it was time to clear out all those things I'd thought might come in useful, some day. So I started in the loft, progressed through each room and finally under the house to the cellar. Everything that had lain unused for years had to go – I wasn't wasteful – I sold some things for nominal amounts and brought happiness to some: a retired farmer and his wife bought a set of cane conservatory furniture for twenty pounds and took it away in a horse box; a retired lorry driver drove all the way up from Newcastle with his friend and bought the antique wood burning stove for a mere fifty pounds.

But mostly I gave things away and brought even greater happiness: a young father collected a cot; refugees got two pine beds; and a middle aged man was thrilled by the old Amstrad computer because it reminded him of his youth.

Then I started on the paperwork and came across old writings, novels half written, scraps of poems – all to be revised, polished, finished – some day. Well that some day is now.

THE POEMS

For my family

Footsteps

I hear the sound of footsteps
Young feet treading ancient stairs
My child straight from her warm bed
Has sought me out to seek
My reassurance

I hear the creek of ancient wood
Old stairs bearing the weight
Of future generations
My child is warm and comforting
We give each other
Reassurance

The stairs are quiet now
The home filled with the sound of peace
My child, blankets tucked, safe and secure
Sleeps deep untroubled
Sleep

Brighton 1970s. Two-year old Lisa frequently crept down the stairs.

———

Something Has Happened

I was watching the television the other day and I saw
Ten thousand men shot dead on the steps of a cathedral
Yesterday I was reading the newspaper and I read
Twenty thousand men and women were clubbed to death
To keep law and order
Today I walked outside and it was perfectly silent
Something has happened to the world
Now even the children have gone

Brighton 1970s.

Out Walking in Sussex

Out walking with my two year old
We met an old lady with an Alsatian dog
The dog lunged at my child, tearing at his flesh
The dog killed my child before my eyes

The old lady looked up and said,
"My dog's life is worth more to me than your child's."

Out Walking in Ireland

Out walking with my two year old
We met a red-faced farmer with his dog
The dog kept his distance, he obeyed commands
The dog herded sheep before my eyes

The farmer smiled at my child and said,
"That's a fine looking boy you've got there.
May God preserve him."

Brighton 1970s.

———

13

The Black, the White, and the Brown

Leonard you're a little black boy
You look like something you see on a marmalade jar
Leonard you're a little white boy
A milky-bar kid without any heart
Leonard you're a little bit white and a little bit black
A worthy oriental gentleman or WOG for short

And so it seems there is no place
for black or white or brown
The world now belongs to some vicious clown,
who plays and jokes with us, hoping, at last,
to find us all heaped together in one communal grave

Brighton 1970s.

A Barren Land

How can I find poetry in this barren land?
Nothing pleases me
The gardens are cultivated with pesticides and weed killers
The houses are unlived in and silent
Trapping their inhabitants in isolation
The people are competitive and cynical
The park is full of dogs people prefer to children

How can I find poetry in this barren land?
Everything is halted and unharmonious
Everybody thinks of themselves first and last
Camaraderie has been reduced to four people
Round a television set
And the children do spelling tests at school
Nothing pleases me
There is no poetry in this barren land

Brighton 1970s.

Moonshine

Day lasts forever on this side of the moon
But on the other
Night stretches into eternity
And so we live our lives
Believing day lasts forever
Feeling we shall never know
The dark side of the moon

Brighton 1970s.

Wimpey House Song

Watercolour houses
on a watercolour hill
Watercolour men and women
live there still
The children swear
and they compare
each other's brand-new bikes
and through the paper-thin walls
disturb each other's nights

And yet
Can you wish for anything better?
Don't you think if could be much worse?

Watercolour houses
On a watercolour hill
Watercolour men and women
Live there still

Brighton 1970s.

Mother Love

My children are the best children in the world
They are the most beautiful, the most deserving
You won't believe me
But it's true

Sometimes my children are an anchor round my neck
Weighing me down, keeping me fixed
You won't believe me
But it's true

My children grow up tall, as I grow old
They are the future
It's true

Brighton 1970s.

Life's Not Like That

It's children fighting over trifles
with mothers screaming vengeance.
It's husbands taking all they can get and more
with wives nagging recompense.

It's rainy days with the cloud hanging
so low that all hope stops before
you set foot outside the front door.

It's getting old and wrinkled
with hope of only more and more days of
Life like this.

Brighton 1970s.

Husband

He destroys me
He captures me in his presence
He overloads me with weighty repressions
He presses me into the dust
I cannot flow
I cannot think free
I cannot be me

but

When he's away
I long for his presence
The smell of his body
The comfort of his arms
The power of his legs
The warmth with which
He surrounds me

Brighton 1970s.

Growing Children

I pity the way they grow
Gradually losing the will to spring
out of bed first thing
in the fresh
morning light.

I pity the way they grow
Horizons gradually closing down
They end as office workers in town
with the chaos thriving
within them.

Brighton 1970s.

A Child's Room

Told to play
Far away
From the adult's day

While outside on the street
The boys aren't neat
What a treat
If this child could play
In the street one day
And feel the joy of gutter companions

Brighton 1970s.

A Children's Room

Full of colours and jumbles of timeless pleasure
Whispering secrets heard only by five year olds
Imagining great Everest conquering feats
Adventurers have played in this room

Here the future is envisaged through lego and a plastic elephant
Here the patterns on the wall weave out security and love
Here as young eyes close and breaths become even
The mother watches and says,
"They're lovely when they're asleep"

Brighton 1970s.

Warm Bread

Fresh from the bakers
Warm in my hands
Carry it home
Eat it alone
Until I grow fat
And dough like

A teaspoon of rice
Tight in brown hand
Carried over hot land
Shared between six
As thin as sticks
And starving

After buying bread at the local bakery. Brighton 1970s.

The Old Images Have Gone

My daughter says she does not want to be
A housewife like me
Grumbling and groaning as I dust and clean

What image will she mould her life upon?
Now the old images have gone

Brighton 1970s.

———

A Miracle of a Person

Every now and again I see
A miracle of a person

Perhaps an old benevolent man
Bright eyes shining in wrinkled face
All dressed up for a day's escape
With grandchildren in hand

Perhaps a happy young child
Haphazardly dressed in unironed clothes
Running along, all rounded limbs
Shouting with the joy of life

Every now and again I see
A miracle of a person

Brighton 1970s. Ian was that toddler.

I Saw a Monkey in a Zoo

I saw a monkey in a zoo sucking at his thumb.
'Ah, poor thing,' they said. 'What he needs is a friend'.

I saw a child in a pram sucking at a tattered cloth.
'It keeps her quiet,' they said.
'She won't go anywhere without it'.

Reduced to such tattered shreds of comfort from old cloth
Envy the monkey in the zoo, at least his needs are known

Brighton 1970s.

Handicap

It's not much fun fishing in this oasis
for one thing the water's not very deep
you can see the fish
there are only a few and
skinny ones at that.

Then there's the shade from the palm tree
well, it's not shade exactly, the tree's old
the fronds are tattered, so
the sun gets through and
burns my naked back.

Even if I do catch the fish
there's the problem of reduced stocks
soon there will be only one left and
then what? I ask myself.
Perhaps it's better not to fish at all.
It's not much fun fishing in this oasis.

Brighton 1970s. In memory of Heiner Pabst.

Middle Class Race

Six foot six the two of them
Children three foot three
Had a big luxurious car
Plenty of money in the bank
Went around with noses in the air
Knowing that they and their kind ruled the world forever

That's the last I heard of them

Brighton 1970s.

Dining Out in Sussex

The garden smells sweet
Is well tended and neat
The people well dressed
And polished
To shine at intellectual
Acrobatics

They see all sides of the question
Have read all the books
Have calculated the mathematics
Have lived, loved and grown old
Yet
May have missed
The vital point
Of it all

After dinner at a professor's house in Lewes. Brighton 1970s.

I'm Alright Jack

In the dark undergrowth
Someone wanders
No flowers here
Just a few poisonous fungi
And a slimy frog

In the dark undergrowth
Someone slips
Cries for help
Just an echo no one listens
And no one comes

In the dark undergrowth
Someone finds
A tree with branches
Just manages to struggle upwards
And find the sun

In the shimmering light above
Someone sees
Birds and butterflies
People laughing in a clearing

And cracking jokes

In the shady forest clearing
Someone drinks
Sings for joy
Hears a calling from the darkness
But no one listens
And no one comes

Brighton 1970s.

A new start; a new person; a new freedom
The most impossible of all impossibilities

A hungry child says:
"They say the world is getting smaller but they are wrong.
It is big, very, very big and far, far out of my grasp."

Brighton 1970s.

English Heritage

I have a heritage sustaining me
and dragging me down.
I know that once kings ruled and paupers starved.
That once some prospered while small boys
cleaned wide Victorian chimneys.
This drags me down.

I have a heritage sustaining me
and dragging me down.
I know that once white men travelled the globe
brought back riches and slaves
built up empires and plantations out of the
sweat and blood of others.
This drags me down.

I have a heritage sustaining me
and dragging me down.
I know that there have always been
those who have noticed,
raindrops glistening on a cobweb,
the marvel of a newborn child
and the green grass growing.

Brighton 1970s.

A World of My Own

I have made a world of my own
filling it with children and the sound of laughter
seeing beauty in an old armchair and
a toddler's bike in the rain

We have planted a pear tree
hoping it will bear rich fruit
there are tomatoes growing on the windowsill
sustaining spinach in the back garden

Blanefield 1980s.

The Meeting

sitting in
meetings
repeating
repeatings
fighting
for fundings
full of concern
for 'The man in the street'

Meanwhile 'The woman in the street' left to her own
devices – there was a meeting in progress – devised an
excellent system whereby she made good and also
helped her fellow women into the bargain.

sitting in
meetings
repeating
repeatings
snoring from boredom
and getting paid
thousands
a year

Meanwhile 'The woman in the street' left to her own devices –
there was a meeting in progress – devised an excellent system
whereby she made good and also helped her fellow women into
the bargain. She was a volunteer worker – there weren't the
funds available to pay her.

Blanefield 1980s.

Her face was flushed
not like the delicate blush
of a rose.
Her smoking was constant
like an old fashioned
factory chimney.
Her mind was alert
like the mind of a fox
that is hunted.
Her manner was abrupt
like an elephant that
has to push its way
through the jungle.
Face,
habits,
mind,
manner
moulded
by the situation.
Her brother
at the police station.
Her mother

making ends meet
illegally.
Her sister
smoking at the
age of ten.

Blanefield 1980s. Inspired by a student I taught at the Jeely Piece Centre, Castlemilk.

Life Cycle

My baby born
Feed from my breast
Find nourishment and rest peacefully
Against my heart

So close and such a part of me

My toddler falls and cries
No other but his mother will do
To soothe his battered knee
He stands alone until some hurt or crisis
Sends him rushing to my side

Still close and such a faith in me

My schoolchild finds the open door
Walks out and closes it behind her
She meets a friend, and, as l watch
They fade into the distance
Heads inclined towards each other
Chatting about their school-day world

Their world exists apart from me

And yet when school ends
She comes home
Warmed to find a welcome
And a place to rest

My son has grown so tall
He thinks he knows all there is to know
And criticises everything l do
He says
My politics and policies are all wrong
I brought him up by a mistaken method
I should have changed the world while he was young

He stands almost alone
And needs me only as a butt
To test and try his theories

For a time it was very quiet here
Not a sound or a whisper of another living soul
I looked in the mirror and saw
My face it was a middle-aged face

And yet I still felt hurt
And vulnerable
Like a teenage girl

My son-in-law brought news last night
My daughter has a brand-new baby girl
We laughed and shouted, drank
A whole bottle of champagne, then
Fell happily into our beds
Eager for the next new morning
And the new life

My grandchild
Rest
In my aged arms
Know
That life is short
Fit only for those who can
Sustain and find
Comfort
In the arms of others

A cautionary note
Found on my doorstep

It was damp
Sodden and trodden upon
The ink had run
And smudged

But despite everything
The smeared words
Unreadable through
Neglect on the doorstep
Despite this I knew
The meaning

I was travelling far
Far from my original
Purpose
I was getting caught
In a circus of
Supposed action
I was becoming

A 'career woman'
There was money
There was power
To be had

'The faint insidious beginnings
of power and greed' it read.

Gartmore 27th December 1989.

———

Far too Fast

Driving along country roads at sixty miles per hour
Far too fast for the narrowness
Far too fast for the darkness
Far too fast for the oncoming traffic
Far too fast for the innocent beast

In the headlights a commotion
Seen in a second
Just enough to apply brakes, stop
Make sense of the scene

A pitiful scene

The young bull or cow?
Lying in the middle of the road
Blood running from its leg
Fear glaring from its eyes
Saliva streaming from its mouth
Struck down by a car

The driver on a mobile phone
No doubt telling
It was not his fault

The beast jumped out at him
He had no chance to stop
His headlight bashed in
The damage to his car, luckily, not extensive

And the beast still suffering in the middle of the road
Suffering more when an impatient driver overtakes
The beast, terror gleaming from
Its eyes in the headlights
Struggles to its feet
Its bloody leg hanging
Swinging limp
It tries to walk

Its pain terrible to watch

But the cars are impassive
Their drivers immune
They must get home
Anyway the cow would be dead meat soon
Minced meat and potatoes

A symbol of our advanced civilisation

Driving home on the Aberfoyle Road, 1990s.

Rollerblading

Rollerblading fast over cobbles
down cold, windswept streets
body racked with vibrations
I pass the people at a pace
see them as a blur
my eyes always on the
bright blue of the far distant
skies and shining snows

It's not that I dislike
warm fires
warm food
warm company
It's not that I haven't dreamt
of riches
of world-wide acclaim
of fantastic success
rather that
the bright blue sky, the white snow
are always in my sights

"Why roller blades?" you ask

They keep you close connected to the ground
You still experience all things human
but at an accelerated pace
and the bright blue skies
and the white shining snows
are always in my reach

Gartmore 2000. After watching Ian rollerblading in Edinburgh.

White Sheep

I drive past white sheep
grazing on white ground
made solid and white
by a deep frost of minus six

Their soft lips
thaw the ice
as they nibble
shrivelled up scraps of grass

They're living life on the edge
and yet it all looks
so beautiful
crystals of frost sparkling
in the low winter sun

The difference between
seeing and feeling
The difference between
my world and theirs

To them

A frozen day with nothing but frozen scraps

To me

A beautiful winter scene

Early morning driving to Glasgow from Gartmore. Winter 2000.

I Used To Be a Wolf

I used to be a wolf
Now I'm a dog
with white hairs on my face

I used to be a wolf
roaming forests and plains
Now I'm a dog
walking down suburban streets

I used to be a wolf
catching and eating meat raw
Now I'm a dog
eating processed food from tins

I used to be a wolf
sometimes cold
sometimes starving in winter wastes

I am both wolf and dog
carrying both
across the centuries

Watching a man walking his dog in Milngavie. Gartmore 2000.

The Virus of Nationalism

Driving to work
I heard it on the radio
a woman speaking in erudite terms
of war
a General speaking of his real experiences
of war
while the blossoms of spring
were sitting pretty on branches
she spoke of the
virus of nationalism
both within and without

Sometimes it creeps up on me
and nips my shin
with razor sharp teeth
I whack it away
with a sharp flick
of the wrist
But it is only partially stunned
always lurking somewhere
in the dark
ready and waiting

to start
a war

while the blossoms of Spring
sit pretty on branches

Gartmore, Spring 2000.

The Information Age

You can't force out poetry
it isn't easily written
like typing out a well known recipe
for sponge cake, for example
www.com can't change that

You can take a shower,
feel the relaxing warmth
warm water rushing
over skin
www.com can't change that

You can shave your legs
and then, when smooth to the touch,
rub in body butter
smelling of almonds
www.com can't change that

But you can send an email
to your grown-up child
over five thousand miles
saying. "I'm going out tonight.
Maybe I'll meet the man of my dreams.
Fat chance! :-)"
www.com can do that

Gartmore 18th March 2000. After sending an e-mail to Lisa, living in San Francisco.

Mini-leech and Super-leech
Went to Work One Day

Mini-leech and Super-leech went to work one day
Asked the employee for all the information
took the information and regurgitated it to
the big boss
who, being a Super-leech herself
took the information and...

And so it went on and on and on...

The employee got little in the way of hard cash
grew paler by the minute
eventually was sucked quite dry
became depressed
was hospitalised and given all the modern treatment
which, as fortune would have it,
did not include leeches

Gartmore 2000. While working at Cardonald Further Education College, Glasgow.

Middle Management

I sit here
amidst
middle management
grey for the most part
in looks
and
outlook

Meanwhile
outside
the sun shines
and no doubt
creativity still grows
without the need
of management

They speak
 of
'top slicing'
of
'portfolio creation'

of
'central pots of money'
of
'material budgets'
perhaps convincing themselves
that they are needed
that they can make things happen

When outside the air smells fresh
the green sits bright on tips of branches
and birds catching the spirit
build nests anew

In a renewed world
could we dispense
with middle management?
or does all this greyness
have its place to play
in reminding us
that sometimes
reality is grey?

Cardonald Further Education College, 2000.

How Did I Get Here

How did I get here?
to this point in time
sitting discussing room allocation
when forty years ago
I imagined joy and light
creativity and colour
a valuing of the living world
instead
creativity is drummed down
to a small space
in a lonely cupboard in my mind
my life consumed
and peopled by others
whose creativity is also
discouraged

or who seem content?
with the status quo
buoyed by their own
images of consequence
deluded by self importance

what energies are required
to rise above all this?
to reach that place
where creativity can walk
with its head high
in Scotland
in Spring
in the year 2000

During a meeting in Cardonald College, Glasgow, 2000.

Life's a Joke to Me

Life's a joke to me
I'm a living joke myself you see
Sitting in a wheelchair day after day
Except this morning when I came out to play

Yes this morning was particularly jokeful
The sun was out and I was hopeful
A friend lifted me out of my old wheelchair
I lay on the grass happy to be there

A passerby came trotting along
Full of good spirits humming a song
He lifted me up and placed me with care
Straight back into my old wheelchair!

Off he went with his good deed done
I was left alone to have some fun
Rolling about in this chair of mine
Laughter splitting my sides – yes life's just fine

After talking to a student in a wheelchair. Cardonald College, Glasgow, 2000.

_____

A Comic Act

I have a pet duck
who hasn't got the feet
for climbing
and yet he will
insist upon trying anyway.

His yellow webbed feet
looking and feeling like soft plastic
trip him at every turn
as he struggles up steps to the back door
for a crust or two
or
seeking out warmth
climbs with much noise and commotion
through the cat flap
into the cellar below the house.

His webbed feet always in the way.
His fat white feathered body, clumsy.
Out of his element.
A comic act in quacking white and yellow
– and yet –

what an inspiration to do more!
For what heights could we attain,
if, like this comic duck,
we tried to reach
beyond our given capabilities?

Could we reach far beyond ourselves?
Could we too do more than life equipped us for?
As this duck does.

Gartmore, Spring 2000.

63

In Pursuit of Happiness

I have tried
to capture happiness
in the first scent of summer
in the smell of snow from far off winter mountains
in the sensual joy of sex
in babies sucking at the breast
in sudden unexpected country sunsets
in driving fast dressed for a date in town
in real laughter amongst real friends
and being alone in complete silence

But if you captured happiness
it would die immediately
its poignant, delicate, shimmering form
squashed
its life extinguished
by the strong-arm tactics of possession
its very nature
fleeting as a raindrop on a spider's web
requiring
we leave it to itself
to chose the moment when
it visits us

Gartmore, Spring 2000.

Now Contentment's Something Different from Happiness

Now contentment's something different
Contentment you can have and hold
Like getting home tired out and
making tea and toast and
sitting relaxed in front of the TV
where life is played out harmlessly
on the small screen

Gartmore, Spring 2000.

———

65

Hanging by a thread
of self belief
How pompous can you get?
How far can you take it before
the thread breaks
or is broken by others?

"Who's the expert photographer
here?" she shouted out
For the 'benefit' of others
For the 'benefit' of her children
For the benefit of herself
Trying to make the thread a rope
strongly, intricately, woven
unravellable, woven, this time, from
an 'expertise' in photography

But you cannot weave from
poor friable materials.
Self belief built from bullying
Self belief built upon deluding others
too small to know better
her children

She will be found out in the end
The expert a mere snapper of dead images
Grown old and grey
Living alone
Her children far away

Gartmore, after overhearing a neighbour, 2000.

Life in the Twenty First Century

A Russian walrus with toothache
cries on the radio.
A dentist from London will treat it.

An old war veteran
asks for ten thousand
to pay for a field in France
littered with his friends' bones
To stop a farmer from plowing it
to plant potatoes

Incongruously I think of
the wondrous nature of the world
made wondrous by kindness
of one creature for another
and by remembrance
of one for another
year upon year

Gartmore, Summer 2000.

A Sense of Distance

sitting in a little room
on a little planet
on an Autumn day
I cry at something
I read in the newspaper

"I haven't an ounce of
distance in me" it read
Something about perspective
or lack of it?
hints at the possible
hints at the impossible
evoking hope and hopelessness
making me cry

Gartmore, Autumn 2000.

KEEP IT REAL
the hoarding said

Reality
What's that?

Is it for example
a cold grey rainy day in December?
or a day of soft grey skies replenishing rain
mingling with yellow green leaves still left on trees
and a warm house to sit in
with a newspaper to read?

Gartmore, December 2000.

Tracings

From engagement ring – to Burnt Norton –
to Ecclesiastes 315

Echoes of the same idea
spreading ripples across Time
from Big Bang to now
time past time present time future

Time passing is what we are
in unremitting, perpetual motion
arriving at our ends too soon

The engagement ring with two diamonds
cut up to make some earrings
for a daughter
time past time present time future

The son part of time past
his future snuffed out one day
on a busy Glasgow Road
Time past, Time past, Time past

What if time past were time present
were time future after all
Ecclesiastes right, Elliot right,
engagement ring vindicated
and Time a place to stroll in
and find the ones we loved?

After the death of a friend's son. Gartmore 2000.

Driving to Work

I catch a glance
out of the corner
of my eye

A tree in bud
two mallards on a wall

My main sights
on the road
ahead

I wonder why?

Driving from Gartmore to Glasgow. Gartmore, Spring 2001.

Run

"Don't run before you can walk"
they say

Why not?
The running's the fun part
you can learn to walk afterwards

Gartmore, Spring 2001.

Late Starter

"I've started too late.
I need three lives," I said.
"Better to have started late than never," he replied.
I ponder the value of all this.

There is something to be said
for being unaware
like the cat asleep
in a spot of sunlight
on the faded rug
or the small, light as air,
blackbird singing
in the Spring sun.
Caring less for beginnings
and ends.
Living only for the moment.

Whereas
We are the past
We are the future
The precious, present, moments
Of no concern to us

Gartmore 2001.

Magical Mystery Tour

On a magical mystery tour
Inspector Morse trail
Or just a bid, desperate almost,
to find a long lost brother

Sitting in a Sheffield pub
Somewhere on the edge
I've ordered fish and chips
to keep me warm
on the descent downhill
to the tiny caravan,
the smallest in the small park

Its windows sealed
Its curtains drawn
tight shut
three teabags thrown
by the bin
a sign of life
perhaps
I've found him here?

On the outskirts of Sheffield. Easter 2001.

Edinburgh Flat

I saw it through the window
A front room with old sanded wooden floors
Antique tiled fireplace, bright yellow walls
A place fit for my daughter
That was all just a glimpse
On a grey cold day
In June
In Edinburgh

And so we bought it mortgaged to the hilt
For a lifetime
And now less than a year later
I sleep in that same room
Its face changed completely by the hope of youth
The yellow walls now purple, the door pink
The moon and the stars captured
Only the fireplace and the sanded floor remain
unchanged
Outlines of continuity
From that day in June

While staying in Ruth's flat in Edinburgh, 4th May 2001.

77

Sunny Saturday in May

"We share this planet between us"
I say to my cat.
The cat shining black in the morning sun
lying purring along my black
velvet covered legs.
Someone shouts disturbing our peace.
A dog has gone missing
"Heidi!" "Heidi!" the dog's name.
The cat not so fond of dogs
stops, listens, then settles
down by my side.
I not so fond of noisy interruption
stop, listen, then return
to my peaceful reverie.

"We share this planet between us"
I say to my cat.
The cat growing impatient,
never a patient cat, grasps my
stroking hand in outstretched
claw!
I shout and threaten.

She runs.

"Ah well, life's not meant to be perfect"

I mutter reproachfully.

Gartmore 2001.

A Hundred Year Old Humpback Whale

A hundred year old Humpback whale
swims onto a northern beach
after one hundred years
in deep oceans
A slumped and clumsy form
laying on a shingled beach
so that if you could roll it over
you would see indentations of
small stones in its ancient skin

The newspaper says
it swam to the beach
to die
– it was very weak
– it was humanely killed
A hundred years spent
swimming across oceans
ended by human hand
on dry land

How can we know
what that whale wanted

More likely, "Air! More Air!"
to give itself a few more moments
Leaving its watery home
to take a chance on land
What did it have to lose?

But in its dying breath
did it realise its mistake?
or, loving the deeps
more than the land
preferred not to be drowned
by its loving watery home?

We will never know
A whale's life is not ours
We breathe the same air
but sing our own
quite different songs

Gartmore 2001.

Flu Virus

there's nothing like a flu virus
for bringing out the worse
in families
reminding you of a genetic
base
you'd much rather forget
the body pared down to
its basics
no veneer of civilisation
when ravaged by flu

and what do I find
is left of myself?
meanness – I kick the cat
vindictiveness – I blame my mother
self pity – I haven't been given a fair chance
sadness – I cry because my children aren't perfect
vainness – I looked at my face and bemoaned it
stupidity – I cannot think clearly
resourcefulness – none, I cannot make a cup of tea
pessimism – absolute

Gartmore. Winter 2001.

"Join the club" she said
As she passed by walking her dog
As I walked mine
In the pouring rain
A friendly gesture
Acknowledgement of similar circumstance

"Fuck the club" I think to myself
Where does this aggression come from?
Is it the Celtic part of me?
The Scottish influence
The fact that 'fuck' is used so much in Glasgow
A routine mode of expression.

Or is it the English in me?
Shunning conformity
Individuality at all costs
No club for me.
No thank you!

Part Scottish, part English
And what about that part that could become American?

Travelling to start anew
In a new continent
As our predecessors did
And what about the African in me?
Earliest of earlier ancestor

Until I am forced to see
Conformity
Attachment to others
And at least admit
The idea of the Brotherhood of Man.

Gartmore 2002.

Glasgow Umbrella

The Glasgow umbrella blown inside out
By driving wind and rain
Has bare twisted spokes
To poke you in the eye

On Being a Mother amongst Other Things

On being a mother
amongst other things
weighing each need
against the other
never getting the balance right

Gartmore 2002.

Falling Moon

I saw a falling moon on a San Franciscan evening
in December
Driving home from a Mexican meal
on Mission
With a talkative Californian woman driving under the influence
of Tequila

At once rooted in the inconsequentialness of activity
and yet attached to the falling moon
A crescent on its back low on the horizon
A symbol of our smallness
and eventual fall

On the way home from a night out with Lisa and Sheila. Written, 85 Watt Avenue,
December 2004.

Crossing Continents

Elephants cross the road in Botswana
And rabbits in England if you're lucky

Size wins in Botswana
You put on your hazard lights and wait

Grey shadowy form crossing slowly

In England the rabbit gets squashed as often as not

There is Plenty of Rain here in Scotland

"They have beautiful camels in Mali
And staggeringly beautiful people
And sleep on the sand
And eat days old meat"
So it's said
On the radio

There is plenty of rain here in Scotland

Gartmore 2006.

If I had a Choice and the World wasn't Racist

If I had a choice and the world wasn't racist
I'd like black skin

I could wear white and look stunning
I could wear bright jewellery and red and yellow dresses

I could plait my hair with glittering beads
And look thirty when I was sixty

If I had a choice and the world wasn't racist

Written when I was sixty (probably). Gartmore 2006.

A New Start

I could gradually clear out all the crap
And start again

I'll begin in the sitting room
Clear out old books
Dust under the settee
And start again

I'll progress to the kitchen
Throw out old pots and pans
Give antique plates back to Oxfam
And start again

Then the children's bedrooms
File away old textbooks
Give away old toys, redecorate
And start again

I'll get to the attic
Stuffed with belongings, not mine mostly
A long lost brother's books
Son's belongings dumped from travels, daughters' pictures
Could I clear them out
And start again?

Gartmore 2007.

Unalloyed Delight

'Unalloyed' I looked it up
'Complete and unreserved' it read

That's what I want
A chance to sing
To fly with youthful bones towards the sun
To see time as something to laugh at
Having plenty of time ahead of me

A purity of delight
A yearning to be young again

Gartmore 2000s.

Two Quilts

One quilt in shades of palest mauve, touching on grey
Like the sweet uncomplicated dreams of the newborn
Fluffy clouds of dreams drifting gently across a sleepy world
Before you learn
Before you discover
Before all those experiences crowd in
Sleep sound
Sleep well
Sweet dreams

Another quilt
No quiet dreams here
Bursts of brightness
Blasts of noise
Light and dark
Black and white
Dissonances of sound
Clashes of colour
Experiences of every hue
Bursting upon your young mind like fireworks in a starlit night
And you now months old create rich dreams
Action packed precursors of a life to live

Gartmore, Scotland & Hartford, Cheshire, 2008. After making two quilts for my
grandson Iain, born 1st June 2008.

A Cardboard Box for Christmas

Given a gift
Wrapped in prime colours
Ripped open the box
Flung to one side

And the gift
My first Christmas teddy bear
Flung aside
Factory made boredom

But the box
Ripped and torn
Held something still
I picked it up

This cardboard box
At first rejected
Opened up possibilities
Of my own making

First I tasted its corners
Joy to sore gums
Lovely to bite on
Reduced to soggy softness

I looked inside
Dark corners
Areas of brightness
Waiting for exploration

I climbed inside
And found a world
Danger and joy
Darkness and light

It came to an end
As all things must
I cried loudly
The box torn from my hands

Inspired by my grandson Iain. Gartmore 2009.

Cushioned

Cushioned by others here in Belize
"I will give you wings.
You do not need to die to be an angel," the groom
"I love you too," the bride

And so it is a celebration of cushioning
Sheltered from fear by human warmth
Happiness spread by song and dance
A wedding party in full swing
Beat out upon a drum

Belize, 15th November 2010.

Footprints

Footprints on my kitchen floor
Dusty grey on white
Dusty white on black
Footprints of my dog

Other footprints long gone
Some gone forever
Footprints of my mother
Two years lost
But never forgotten, as they say

The sun comes out
And I'm reminded of my grandson
Making footprints five thousand miles away
Stepping out into the future
Footprints in the sands of time

Gartmore, July 2011.

Make Me a Shoe

Make me a shoe
I can run in

Make me a shoe
Soft, pliable, comfort

Make me a shoe
Strong, waterproof, enduring

Make me a shoe
Everlasting

Gartmore, May 2017.

Did I Write a Poem Once?

Did I write a poem once?
About a Mum for all seasons
Who was there for every main event

Did I write a poem once?
About frosted grasses sparkling rainbows
In a winter sun

Did I write a poem once?
About a forty year old son
And how much he had done

Did I write a poem once?
About birds singing in spring
Among the yellow blossoming brooms

Did I write a poem once?
About the resilience of my daughters
Through life's traumas

If I didn't I should have

Gartmore, Spring 2017.

Clear Out All the Crap

When a friend dies
It's time
To clear out
All the crap

All those things you thought
You couldn't do without
That might come in useful
Some day

But the end of all days
Is getting closer
And if that, old chair, old table, old stove
Hasn't come in useful yet?

Well then, I'll grasp the moment
Before someone else, a relative, most likely
Comes and clears out all the crap
After I'm just a face on a photograph

Gartmore, April 2017 in memory of Margaret Arrol, who died on International
Women's Day on March 8th 2017, and who was always unsentimental.

Also by Sue Bates

A series of humorous, illustrated, books for 5 to 8 year olds:
The Bold Worm; *The Independent Ant*; *The Lazy Bee*;
The Flying Caterpillar; and *The Carefree Ladybug*.

Supersleuths in Space aka Intergalactic Posties,
a novel for 8 to 11 year olds.

Penny Whistle the Bread Bin Mouse,
a limited edition book for 5 to 8 year olds.

What is a Watt? The Adventures of Five Light Bulbs,
an educational, humorous, illustrated book for 5 to 8 year olds.

Leopard in the Grass, a light hearted novel
about a woman, a dog, and a leopard.

Little Old Lady, a novel following the exploits of a woman
determined to escape the confines of old age.

www.bothy-publishing.com
enquiries@bothy-publishing.com

www.ingramcontent.com/pod-product-compliance
Lightning Source LLC
Chambersburg PA
CBHW071820020426
42331CB00007B/1558